ORIENT

Orient

FIRST EDITION

Copyright © 2018 Nicholas Gulig
Printed in the United States of America

ISBN 978·0·9963167·8·1
DESIGN ≈ SEVY PEREZ
Text in Verlag HTF and ITC Garamond Std

INTERIOR COVER PAINTING
Yukimi Annand

BOOK IMAGES
Ian Wallace

PAGE 107 IMAGE, BOTTOM
"Lake Photograph," Tony Gulig

This book is published by the

Cleveland State University Poetry Center
csupoetrycenter.com
2121 Euclid Avenue, Cleveland, Ohio 44115-2214

and is distributed by

SPD / Small Press Distribution, Inc.
spdbooks.org
1341 Seventh Street Berkeley, California 94710-1409

A CATALOG RECORD FOR THIS TITLE IS
AVAILABLE FROM THE LIBRARY OF CONGRESS

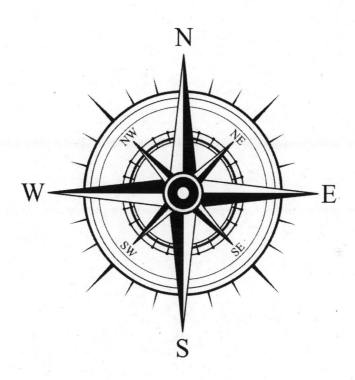

ORIENT

~

NICHOLAS GULIG

TERRORED INTO, THE I IS NOT AS WE IMAGINED IT ‖ OTHER THAN, OR

ELSEWHERE ‖ A DESERT RENDERED THROUGH THE VIOLENCE OF ITS OPENING

TABLE OF CONTENTS

An Image of the Book in which I Hear You

How can we remain beneath a single roof? / When there are seas
between us, and walls, deserts of cold ash…
~ *Khalil Hawi*

Through the ear, we shall enter the invisibility of things...
~ *Edmond Jabès*

AN IMAGE OF THE BOOK IN WHICH I HEAR YOU

If there is standing water in the desert. If there is water and I am standing
over it. Staring down into the murk

or mirror of the pool.
If I am breathing. If I can see myself in the oasis.

If I am speaking and there is water
and you are there.

If you are also speaking. If we can hear across
the water, our voices

carrying in opposite directions,
our voices carrying. If our languages unspool in blue drifts

against the distance, escaping reticence.
If the distance of our reticence

is false. If it isn't crossable.
If we cross it anyway.

Who will carry us? If our narratives erase us.
If our histories return to us

as names. If we are living
in the error of our alphabets. If the centers of the letters

hurt. Master, Stranger. What is water,

where is water safe

if solitude displaces us? If we are homeless, finally,
each of us. If we wander past

each other, our faces moored
to their reflections,

the edges wrecked. Is it imaginary?
If the images we make

remake us. If there is mercy
in us. If our speaking

changes, and we, ourselves,
are changing, making. If we are made

in the image of the other. In ambiguity and contradiction.
If we consent

        to not be solitary. If we imagine we are somewhere.
                If there is shore

ORIENT

Spring arrived and lasted. Thousands gathered in the capital. Though you were terrified, you grew excited. Your daughter asked to play among the signs and flags below you in the alleyways. You told her "later." You pointed to the people; they were beautiful. You told her "listen." You heard your neighbors there, your relatives. A man in a black jacket looked up at you and smiled. He gestured with his hands; he shouted. You couldn't hear him. Your daughter waved. "Who is that?" she asked. But then her voice, among the others, drowned, there in the opening between you.

SOME CACOPHONIES

One begins by saying, "the world is what surrounds us." When listened to, when repositioned in the body, surroundings resonate; they shake. Objects are their noises

Translated into language and recorded, the memory of noise exists within a history and speaks, a wave of sound that moves beyond itself and travels. Over time, this grows into a roar

Imagine that it measures us, a confluence of messy energies transgressing flesh and borders. One could call this an "occupation." A body languaged into politics. One could say, "erased"

As noises drift across the landscape they enter the thought and fabric of the human form, mark a space of difference between a subject and its object. This distinction subjugates, imposes order, a projection that defines the project of pornography as well as capital, the crawl of empire

When mapped by noises that desire it, the mind becomes an interstice expressed by violence, sound, and alteration. To hear this is to hear the cry of injury. Conflict is transformative

Occurring in both the spirit and the flesh, the change that noise creates is radical. The human subject sinks into its injury. The distance between "here" and "there," the "self" and "other," the "sacred" and "profane," collapses fundamentally, even if only for a moment. New noises break into the world. One is wrought by the totality. A person puts an ear against the ground and listens. One is overcome

Pronounced across an opening, the act of listening constructs a bridge that binds a single space. This despite the distance and the violence of difference

A vital emptiness, the field between polarities begins to open outward, slowly like a desert, a tract of sand through which the noise we make begins to wander. Language is the record of this wandering. Books are echoes

Often terrifying, the noise reverberates against the tiny bones inside the ear and writes them in the image of its occurrence. Names are also noises, their sound a sense and self that we make visible and occupy and claim

Others add to the cacophony. Their voices find us. There, in the interior, I is I no longer, incessant texture spiraling in all directions. A loud contingency. A whirlwind

Here, the noise arrives across the desert carrying the history of these distortions. Attempting to internalize the sound of forces far away a person runs the risk and violence of reduction. War becomes consumable. A strange pornography

Everyone is watching, waiting. In homes and offices, in universities. We wait in cars, in lines, at banks. In restaurants beside our families. It overwhelms a person's thinking, this cacophony. The sound of things unearths

The sound of things unearths; the noise creates an impasse. One ignores the potentiality of objects, the possibility of song

Listening is different. Mind and body meet with their surroundings. Beyond circumference, thinking moves into the storm

There, in the unstill center, the noise becomes a patterning that one envisions as a gift, a vital static. Art is the investigation of this static, the performance of its recovery and transformation. Disorder is a source

A person listens to the din of distant energies in order to rework them, a translation of the noise of others into form, an aesthetic framed by awe, or ache, or apathy. Art has already walked the violent path of apathy, a road that splits the land in half, delineates "the west" as Occident, "the east" as something else. This path leads a person backward to the shadow of the valley of the self, the very source of empire

Empire exists. A person dreams to walk into the wilderness. To place an ear against the ground and listen. To scream the names of others into sand

Say this screaming resonates, a kind of culmination. One begins to recognize the shape and form of other faces, a sea of voices crossing states and sand and nations, becoming politics, the boundaries of self and other, bewildered past the singular, the sound of it, of making

You sensed the weather of the movement changing. The students painted their demands upon the wall. They were erased. At Omari they drowned a mosque in gas. A fire started. Your husband was arrested and a woman you grew up with was beaten. On the television, you watched the soldiers turn their rifles on the crowd; the crowd roared. Buildings trembled. You closed your windows, doors. There was no escaping it. When the tanks were called, you hid beside your daughter in the basement. You began to teach her English. "You will need this. There will come a day," you said, "and you will need this."

BOOK OF CROSSING

1.]

The Syrian Desert does not belong to Syria. Oil lines bisect it. Its borders pass through the kingdoms of Saudi Arabia, Jordan, and the republic of Iraq.

What defines a desert is its opposite. Each year, on average, 125 millimeters of rain fall on an area of approximately 200,000 square miles, most of which evaporates.

No human has ever crossed this portion of the world without the aid of animals, recently machines.

In 2009, near the Catholic monastery of Deir Mar Musa, a team of archeologists unearth a structure dating back to the early Neolithic period.

Native to the area for nearly twenty centuries, the Bedouin have no record of these ruins, no memory. It is believed the ancients housed their dead before themselves, traveling great distances each year to mourn as a community

2.]

Increasingly familiar, the once uncharted territory of the desert's face exists primarily as reminiscence. Our earliest accounts of these topographies include the collective imaginations of nomadic tribes, partial narratives inscribed as memory on excavated tablets bearing signs extinct for centuries. These markings list the names and natures of gods and spirits native to the area.

Before Islam defined "the east," Christianity "the west," a multiplicity of vibrant histories interacted in a vital, empty space.

Experienced as sand and gravity and glass, history is the measurement by which a people express the possibility of their connection against the fact of their erasure

3.]

An invention of the Egyptians, the hourglass measures time in granulates of sand, portions of the desert lifted up and carried across its surface in the hands of slaves from conquered nations.

This sand funnels slowly through an opening, charts the movement of the earth around the sun, two spheres connected by the same energy that pulls the desert downward through a hole.

Formed by accident, the glass through which the sand descends first appeared in either Syria or Mesopotamia. Humans melting metal, making weapons

4.]

Glass results from an eruption of the earth's interior, toward and through its surface, as sand that lightning strikes by chance and changes.

Lightning meets the surface of the earth approximately 100 times per second, a brief and volatile connection.

As wave and particle, the light that strikes the desert passes through an even vaster space, a substance claimed in the Old Testament and the Qur'an as void or chaos, both of which are nothing and predate the earth, its violent history, and hold it

5.]

Discovered in the summer of 2005, in Syria, the bones of a previously unknown species of megafauna camel show the animal to have been slaughtered by early humans while drinking from a pool.

Dating back approximately 100,000 years, the remains were not originally identified as belonging to the dromedary.

Present at the excavation site, a young American removes layers of dust and sand from the hoof of the giant ungulate. The desert sets behind him.

Years later, this same man will be arrested for attempting to firebomb a research facility at Michigan Technological University.

Sitting in Ohio, in his cell, the American remembers clearly the wind that lifted the desert up and set it down again in drifts, recalling, with a calm and dangerous nostalgia, the pound of dirt and bone still sleeping after centuries.

All this time the light attached by light,
there between his hands

Tens of thousands gathered in Damascus and Daraa. Even the non-believers joined the people. After Ghouta, it became impossible. The country had erased itself in chemicals, in shells. Still, the dissidents continued disappearing. You felt their deaths upon you. Somehow you accepted it, the weight accumulating. Accruing ache, their faces changed to names within your mouth, then nothing. You could not describe it. To do so you would need a looser word, a larger god to guide you.

THE LANDSCAPE OF THE SECULAR

I was 21 when the towers fell. My aesthetics failed me. It was a Tuesday. I was asleep in a basement. I hadn't been to college. I lay in the dark. The walls were spray-painted. The air, poisonous. I was 21. The floor was cold. I had no money. My friends took care of me

In the mornings I ate for free at a small café beside a river. I listened to the radio and wrote. My friends, they cared for me. My aesthetics failed me. The river ran through the center of my city. I was 21. It was morning

I was American. Through the ceiling, the distant static of the television. I had no money. The static started in the room above me. It approached. A wave washed over me, almost totally. I ignored it

My aesthetics failed me. The night before I drank in a bar on Water Street. Music, and the sound of voices rising, falling. My friends, living. They paid for me. They helped me. I was 21. I vomited. I returned to bed. I laid in the dark. I was alone

Years later, I remember walking up the stairs and waking. I rubbed my eyes. I looked at the television. The mirror of the river, or a screen

A single plane appeared above you, a streak of silver passing through the clouds and lasting. Your daughter pointed and she shouted and she learned. You reached for your belongings.

BROADCAST

There was, within the house, a funeral.
It began beyond me. Audibly. Though it was not
my own, did not decrease me physically,
I felt it happening. Everywhere around me,

happening, the broadcast took the shape of suffering
and changed it. It made it public. Images
of mourners, to and fro on television, erased
a necessary difference. Their sense [a kind of sadness

edged against despair] sparked the desert into tribes.
I shrank from my surroundings. The nearer
trees and forests shook within the light
of brighter weaponry. Which was adjacent to

and did appear within the mirror of its spectacle.
It was an ancient light. I raised my voice
to it. I trembled. My trembling
became me. Almost utterly. Still, it failed

to reach the abstract marker
of a specter. And did or didn't change itself
into a book. I couldn't tell. I turned
the television off. The funeral remained

a funeral. A range of many nights I painted
in its aftermath an alphabet
remembered partially in the dark [its aperture

a plethora of stars approaching
their disclosure] and failed to resurrect a self

that wasn't sectional. I was I
who ended. And spoke instead another's name
to press against that precedent. Which superseded me,
and tore itself, without my help, from song

What to carry with you? What you to carry?

BOOK OF ORIGINS

1.]

In the beginning the sound of "I" was given into, a certain emptiness existing. Caliphate, or sky. It wasn't even morning.

Because the world and weight of human thought as it exists exists in actual relation to a context experienced primarily as physical, translation is necessity.

[We were a garden once.] [The limits of
our language.] [God]

2.]

When I was ten, I watched the war begin on television. I was at a party. It was a birthday party. We were listening to the radio. I called the station and requested music. They played it. We sang along. I called again. We danced. I was drinking Coca-Cola. I was eating ice cream. I was American. My friends were all around me. I walked upstairs. In the living room, parents watched a sitcom in recliners. The news came on. I sat on the couch. The news washed over me. Quite specifically, I remember the green-bright traces of artillery, the way the night above the desert trembled. I had never seen a war. I wept. I was at a party. It was a birthday party. My father took me home

3.]

Agree or disagree. A person prays alone within a circle made of talk and is political.
This is one of several narratives existing in the contentious space of borders erected
to delineate the real and unreal

fact of difference. [Limits, edges,
frontiers, flowerbeds, etc.]

These are not the same, although, after centuries of warfare, one begins
to question the extent.

I used to think that it was possible to turn away.

As if for a long time. As if from difference our lives erase themselves
and seethe again within the exit

of an artwork. Entered and expanded and expressed, the seeds of an alternative, or
night. "No one carries us."

There are things we sing
among [to see]

4.]

It was summer and we were driving as a family. My mother and sister slept in the backseat. A song came on. The stars

were out. My father
turned it up.

It was late and we were looking for a campsite.
The music was familiar.

I had heard the song before in a movie about a war. I asked my father if he remembered, and he did. I asked if he'd been drafted, if he had fought. He said he was, but that he hadn't. He kept his eyes on the road. The song continued. The road was dark.

I asked him why. He took my hand. The night and song continued. The road grew darker. He was my father

5.]

An originating energy, sunlight passes through the vacant static that surrounds it, a bridge of gold suspended in the air above a setting draped in sand. This connection spans the spectacle between the landscape and the sky, the real and the imaginary. One looks because one must. The world returning in the aftermath. One looks to look away

6.]

"Of adolescence with my father,"
the trees in the gray
lake, shaking
their disturbances, the birds
believing us, his brother
echoing an owl
home across
the water, bringing it
to tree, again
proven, our volition
voiced in August
ash, in whirl
and wash of white
blue ache, the sky
in Canada we called,
were called to
yearly, every summer
the days' perennial
advance across
the continent, a compass
pointing us
to shore, a path
in the forest
opening, his fragments

there, but only
barely, an incandescent
blur, the waves
returning, his scattered form
an old direction
traced, our time together
leaving, a certain stillness centered in
our language, leaving

7.]

Aspiring to meet what it is not, the mind begins beyond its edges. This desire forms the invisible dimensions of a cage in which the distance between a person's freedom and the atrocity of actions claiming to defend it acquires a meaning one did not imagine

8.]

The dead do not come back.
I speak to them

and through them.
To bring you

closer. I speak
to wrench the water from

our names [Desert / Sphere] [Eros
Ultimatum] [Raincloud / Desert] [Morning / A militia] [Broadcast / Reason]

[Shoreline / Vision]
[Beam / of Terror] [Men / Geometry] [As pets

Diaphanous] [The desert
Akbar]

[Allahu / as Limit] [Image / Thing] [State of
Center] [Fear / as Other] [Art

A locket, silver. A pair of passports wrapped in plastic. A syringe. A
bag of marshmallows. Soap. A toothbrush. The Qur'an. Bandages.
A map of Greece, folded. A yellow raincoat. A letter, folded. Tylenol.

THE PATH OF APATHY

Artisan or citizen. The war erases "us" and singing changes nothing. This is one of several narratives in which an aesthetic fails to render, or make better, or explain. There are other ways of saying this, but these, too, despite sincerity, become commodity. The world is made of things

Painted broadly, the noise a person makes
contributes to, and therefore is,
atrocity. I want to say this kindly, from the heart [its center pulling
inward, pulsing] but here, immediately, the words
fall out and fail within the borders of their argument. It is difficult to tell
from where exactly our language comes
from nothing

and where it lives
precisely

Say, for example, the experience of others exists primarily as a vague impression on the horizon. Empathy is like this. The love that is the bottom of the self as it exceeds the flesh and spills into the desert of another life must do so having listened to the scream dissolving at the edges of its end. Who is speaking

there among the photographs and rubble
torn from stone?

Torn from stone, the mind cannot define itself in the face of these events. Agree or disagree. Akin, perhaps, to capital asserting dominance, a form of "fuck" I call myself into the currency of ache. Here
and there. You and I, etc. [subject,

object]. The noise exceeds its culture and exists. Amid the weight
and war of privilege, I am thinking first, "have I eaten,
have I slept." The world goes on

like this. The days and longer hours. The weight of seconds. As difference continues to exert itself. As difference
continues. [Green and yellow-green against the landscape,

a cloud of chlorinated gas disperses
at the edges of the desert.] Moving inward from a distant point

on the horizon. Occurring in the fallow pasture of an afterthought. A person blinking. Stranded in the center

of a market. Existing at the edges
of a town

Journalists appeared in groups. They carried cameras, microphones. They spoke into equipment. Questions surfaced. The cameras recorded everything. They recorded nothing. The desert moved your form across a screen.

SOME PORNOGRAPHIES

Accessible the light of "I" was brutal.
I couldn't help myself. The room
became a screen. I turned it
on. A wilderness replaced me.
Totally. As when the new geometry
of wealth became an era, wrung
a sudden violence from a square in front of me
erupted. There, the screen was multi-
valent. A presence pressed
a self into a crevice, not
a politics, a person. Beginning in Afghanistan,
a war of forms defines the fight
as technical. Was never even radical, the hard positions
cored and punctured through

It wasn't ethical, the aperture agape, a new
cacophony of raw material. The world
is only part material, the arts
are martial, total, the whole
is transcendental. Here and there
I am, it's over now, new champion. How to feel
a champion. When Inger died
the economy became emotional. The alphabet
was evangelical. I had to finish off
myself within the ache of an
effect, its effervescent ending. Beautiful
like that the ankles lashed upon
a screen avoids the self
in which the war is ever brilliant, is contrapuntal

Describe the screen to me by being
partially erased your name
is not its weight
in capital. I don't believe
that we escaped the weather,
ever. It wasn't close
or even closeted, our prettiness
a pettiness erupting inward
moves the eye to several
images of holes, the mouth's abrupt
geometry, a symmetry of she is what without
the self a distant oracle becomes
its pubis. Centered in a public space the internet becomes
a surface. I turned it on, the wilderness

It turned me on. I couldn't help it, he was standing
radiant. Even it, what was it, there,
that it existed, pulsed
and pushed into a mouth's
vocabulary. The her
of here was distant, openly
apart that she and I are similar except for
history, a story told upon the body is
a target, like, totally a market.
Radical the categories choking I
am commentary under images of feet.
So many kinds of interacting in a single
orifice the night I am, that pleasure is. The mind
has made its narrative, existing it desires

This morning I would like to thank
the loud republic.
Without a history of domination
I couldn't be or want
to put my fingers
there, where it, a mouth, is academic, a crevice
stitched together by a dialect,
the alphabet, or drone. Same as wealth
is white, is whitening the new December
sky, a cage surrounding you
should be ashamed, American,
except that we are pulled
by many distances, a part into its pieces,
perfectly. Place your palm into your bicep. Listen

Open up your eyes, same as weather, wealth
is like I love the way you look inside me
there are currencies, a mixing of
the disciplines within a common opening, our reason
caged inside its name, just say it,
says a man, my name, your eyes I want them
open, look at me, the world
which I have hurt is not
what it began against, was not replaced
or spoken through an opening. Of forms
for what a woman wanted as
becomes, the brightest red awash beneath
the lights, the fight defined by heart, by heartlessness.
It isn't natural. The chin is human, holding up against intention

Someday soon I'd like to have a daughter.
The thought of her and then the single
shape a cage becomes
when closing. Lock the door, there
is only me, I've never been
more ready, this is not Afghanistan, a landscape
wrapped in cellophane, the self in light
of its computer. Still,
I want to have a daughter. I want for her
a name to be its music, to say beyond the poem
that it has mattered
somehow. Her mother's voice,
a form of care which moves
and doesn't move. Beyond the scope of politics

Politics exists because economy.
When Inger died in January, the snow existing.
The economy exists because "I want to be
inside you, darling." The Dow
Jones Industrial Average. Afghanistan.
Afghanistan exists, and Syria, our civil difference
witnessed and returned
to us, a distant presence speaking in the waves.
The passion of the terrorist
exists [which terrorist], and so the war
is indescribable, here
in the interior of glades the internet existing,
expressing ache. We gathered in a room and read
the alphabet together in a circle. Privilege, privilege exists

This is what a person does
when poetry is schools. It took me months
to render my technique. The scope
of these polemics, Thee, the air that we inhale
exhausts us, chemical
it clings to bricks a person grips
her ankles, holds together
mostly, a camera's discrete invisibility
existing, maybe we are monkeys
made of money, weaponry
and talk, a language pressed upon
a landscape made of forms for pleasure, what
is pleasure for, it takes existing
in the present tense, a finger not a flower, but a fist

In awe again a narrative in rags to riches forms
the ache and molds it over
in the image of our making, made
to wander, wonder. Thus parade,
thus patriarch, the strange material of suffering,
a voice that rises from the crowd
is on its feet, is roaring, rather vaporous. A wealth
of colored lights and not a weakness over
whelming leaves the record
written over, script or
scripture, in any case a structure
turned into its nature, there, two men turning
circles in a cage. Thankfully, alas. Make me real again, dear artisan,
"bewilderment as a poetics" and a politics. Hold me, Arianny

How to say it right? The desert of an opposite
in rags of light as violence, maybe,
yes. Vision is diverse, the I, its class and clamor
obvious, surreal. That it exists,
is here, its emptiness
negates us. Grant forgiveness,
justice, yes, or mercy. Maybe mercy
or return. Again we reconcile. No one
carries us. A country raw as sand is real
and deadly as a refuge.
We turn away. Turning inward,
east at certain times where it, the light of
day which rests upon the factual
expanse of forms, all surfaces, it rises, there beyond intention

A week before he left, the memory is clear, the image perfect. It was a Saturday. You were standing in the doorway of your living room. The air was warm. Your husband turned to you, and in the inconsistent light he spoke your name.

OMPHALOS

Center, season, cell. Some days all a person does is string the noise into a circuiting. It isn't actual, the fact of thought a field or page of snow enfolded in the creases of the desert, in the cold. Some days fracture in the aftermath. Like years sometimes, like months of numb subtraction, a language learned by route to link occurrences, the aberrant connections, causes. It's getting difficult. The act of thinking webs a difference, a sentence. The words, and then the world, turn back. It isn't accurate. The field evaporates. "Stranger, are you near me?" Despite discrepancy, no sun, nor salt, nor sky can cease enough to render what's interior. Is it wrong to make this up, to speak the world of things without a means to sing that one is listening? Still, it isn't audible until it trembles, tenors through and terrors. A sound pronounced to live inside of, tethered to a death-thought, scattering. The season loosens everything and shakes. Summer, then surrender, a wish for color, winter. I can't remember. Days that never happened, their shape and resonance, the refuse of our variance. Difference is built. The weight of what has left escapes its strange containment. Blue, the blue dark opening, spilling over everything. Edges wisped in light, far particle. It isn't practical, it's stated. Some days vanish in the overlap. The ground itself grows restless, iridescent, bent. Days of rain, of remedy. Talk and circumstance. I had thought for once to simply say it was enough, that it, whatever is, would be there, an exit opening to others, an entrance opening. Cave or covenant, shore or shorelessness. Together we have gathered, errored inward at the water of our end, dark river. Such rushing there, such rising. Into emptiness, rising. Into happiness, as some have said, "in dark again," companion. And so it is that one begins to echo outward. Into openness, a promise. Joy and empathy. The eventual erosions. Love. The receding back, the fall. The falling back. To where, to when, to who. It's getting difficult. Again the sky resists. The ground and what comes after. Matter into mourning. Into shade and ache. Into acre. "This is the sound of the faith a person makes of things." And from them, a form of drift, a weathering, despair. For once I spoke aloud and then believed the point around which turned the world that wasn't there, made true the actual erupting inward of the visual. It made an avenue of sense. Snow fell. It made an avenue of nonsense. Then and only then did I explain myself to no one in particular, performing less than perfectly the aperture of space within my name, its strange arrangement, a monument. There, for a moment, despite the times I lived within the price and privilege of, despite material, its raw pronouncements ever present, the pattern of the real and more than real, I swear I saw a self, mapped upon a plane, vast transparencies, a pure capacity for wonder, grief. Then, surpassing rhetoric, the thought the plane surrounded, drowned to nothing and became

The sun upon the buildings appeared to shake them as you approached the city's edge. Hours blurred. The sky, too, blurring, became the smoke which rose to meet it. People moved among their histories. You took your daughter by the hand. She spoke and failed to speak and spoke again the names of neighbors, and of family, and friends. Objects were their noises.

SOME APOSTASIES

1.]

In central west Wisconsin, a pair of rivers rose as separate streams and met. The city built a park around the confluence, the water intertwined and often shining, the shoreline wooded and kept up.

Where I was born, raised among the farmers and the forests and the punks. I left

2.]

Waking up I stepped outside and called the noise "occurrence." In opposites,
performing radically

the old complexities. As when a living system disassembles
under scrutiny. Is dominant

in shifts [a process
by which a wearing down becomes

reduction] [excavation
and relief]

3.]

I was young and walking in the wilderness.
My friends were all around me.

We had driven there.

White sands blistered in the bright light.
We sat in a circle,

taking drugs.
Everyone was living.

We climbed the dunes and danced.
Brown and floral white, my girlfriend's linen dress swarmed around her

in the hot wind. The bombs were far.
She was intelligent

4.]

Indebted to the subject and the object simultaneously, to that which lives and
breathes within the body

and beyond it, the work that is a gift
negotiates polarity.

Both inward toward its center
and also outward in the direction of its opposite, it isn't possible to say exactly

where the desert ends and where a different word begins to name the climate more
correctly. [Some red

around the edges of the solitary
rocks.] Rather vaporous, a voice estranged within the inconsistent

                                                  light. I heard it [it was there]

5.]

Police found us, closing in from all directions. They took away our drugs and Jessica went with them.

They let us go. We waited

6.]

On average, a grain of sand weighs approximately 0.0000044 kilograms.
The heart, and not the mind, is muscle.

It's beginning to feel a lot like I'm at fault
for something far away.

For example: the total weight of blood that wells within the mouth is or is not
comparable to the same amount of blood spilling in the culturally contested space
of countries

[connected to,
composed]

7.]

The memory is clear, the image
perfect. We were sitting in the middle of the desert

in a circle, waiting. We were American.
The sun came down

around us. Our aesthetics
failed us. A dark speck

on the horizon, Jessica came walking back.
She was alone. We ran to her

across the dunes.
We wept.

And the wind picked up
from somewhere far away. I felt it. It was all

around me. Everywhere around me.
I could almost breathe it. It carried toward us [sand]

8.]

Insofar as one [and thus the war] is often distant as a result of physical location, class, race, religion, and nationality, the anxiety of attempting to express compassion is, in large part, dependent on the extent to which the speaker isn't being bombed

9.]

Agree or disagree. We drove for hours in the late light. A song came on the radio, the music glistening against our insides. Everyone was living. I closed my eyes. The desert disappeared,

or we did. How could I have known then what passed between us as we waited, there in the interior? [The verbs we were

when we were younger. The nouns
we have become]

The city ended and you left it. The two of you, a backpack filled with things. Past Damascus, you paid a pair of men who placed you in a car. You drove in silence.

DAYBOOK

It's October in the Midwest and I'm trying to remember clearly what you were wearing, the expression of your daughter's face before she turned from the reporter.

In Wisconsin, a yellow static changes in the air.
I wonder if you're living.

Where I am, my daughter waits for winter. This snow will be her first. In the mornings, she looks beyond the window.

Where are you?

Here, in the imagination, the world is made of words and through them. I spell the names of things.

So what to do about it?

Imagine I believed myself. Would that protect us? That the mind is matter, that so very little matters anymore but matter.

The longer that I take, the more I work, the less it feels as if you even happened. As though I stand today as I have always stood, speaking without permission in a field you never were.

I turned the television off. I listened
and you spoke.

So what to do about it?

Every time a person with a name I'll never know gets blown up in a world I know I'll never live in, the desert reappears and interrupts the broadcast.

So what to do about it?

I press my ear against materials. I speak of ghosts and through them. If you are near me, tell me. If you are anything at all.

What is violence for if not for falling
far away from people?

I'm beginning to think the war. I'm making weaponry. Imagine with me.
I should like to think the river

Looking out the window, looking up, you thought of those who never made it through the desert, who fed their children grass in plastic cups, and you ignored them. You passed a woman praying in the street. Your daughter stared at her. The air was concrete. You rolled the window up and kissed her. You wrapped her father's scarf around her shoulders.

BOOK OF ERROR

To see and fail to speak from far
away of seeing, to go about
a life, to write to
friends and of them,
to begin within
their names, to wish them well
and end in yours, sincerely,
to drive to work
in a green car singing,
to have insurance, to listen
to the radio, the county
road in autumn,
the light collected
in the maples, in the birches,
beautiful, to mouth
the words of others,
to believe them,
to feel their language
is your own, to own them
momentarily, to feel ashamed
of owning, to stare
into the open
windows of your house,
to stand beside
your wife, in the center
of your yard, living,
breathing, in the middle

of October, the leaves
around you, everywhere
around you, to watch your daughter,
to listen to her laughter
fill you. From far away
across the yard, it fills you.
And then to know within the poem
the noise that other
people make
when suffering. Enough
to love them, to wish them well, you needed
them imagined. You made
them up, the people.
What are people?
And so it was you came
to speak alone, a soul composed
beyond the finite boundary
of an ethics. Etched
into an opening and closing
space, the sound of "it" compressed with "it is not,"
their echoing, your ache

Morning met the ocean. Red light, gold. They divided you in groups. Families measured their belongings. Standing at the shore, its edges breathing, the waves around their ankles, breathing.

MEDIUM

1.]

The origin of utterance is breath, the lung a kind of logic pulled beyond itself and traveling like water. Coming and going, pushing outward, back. Progression and revision and return. This is the momentum, the rhythm and the life. To speak is to participate. To articulate the ocean, wind

2.]

The air that enters us is not significantly discernible from the air that moves across the landscape. The landscape changes in immediate relation to the wind. The crawl of sand across the desert over time, the movement of the dunes, erosion. In this way, the body also experiences a change, is moved by what it's moving through

3.]

The medium through which a person speaks to make the world transforms itself upon pronouncement. One can say this. When I push a button on my machine the alphabet emerges in a field of strange illumination. As the script appears, the field begins to darken. Erecting signs for sounds that point to objects in the world, the self accumulates its diagrams. This, in turn, creates a second world. The self multiplies. When placed correctly in specific sections of the field, the alphabet manipulates the field's identity, determining the shape and resonance of the world which then appears before me. Today, for example, I type "September," I type "tower," I type "fall." A place and point in time appears which I remember, quite specifically, but my memory, as well as the objects in it, trembles into talk. That was years ago. This, too, is a form of transformation

4.]

Looking back, it feels inevitable. The towers fell. The war continues happening. An ache begins to blink within the body. I type "pornography" and the field becomes the image of a woman. Urge or urgency. The performance of these actions within an opening immediately made present occurs primarily as a rendering of signals exerted without regard for sex or consequence, the world within the word that changes it

5.]

In time, a rendering whose main objective is the domination of the body by another body, of a country by another country, arises as one of many possibilities within a context that conceives the souls of others as either separate from the human form or all together nonexistent. A person has a choice. The extent to which the image of the woman in the field is, or is not, discernible from the woman herself—her fear, etc., her ability to love, etc., her history—becomes the measure by which a person then decides if one is singular. Empathy, like the very acts of violence that make it necessary, must be imagined. The fate of others now depends on one's ability to be a maker, to create and then maintain a living faith in the vibrant, vital space of overlap. Between the world that is and the world as one envisions it, a multiplicity of fictions, the miracle of fact. At once the desert, which exists between localities, and the ocean, the ground a portion of the sea expanding, a small oasis in the sand

Blue and gray against the distance, your daughter's scarf begins to twirl across her shoulder like a flag. You are waiting in the water, sand. Will she remember this? The beach is like the desert, opening. She has never seen the sea.

SOME IDENTITIES

Having never seen the sea, having only ever seen,
the sea appears unusual. I remember

waking up and making, imagining a world in which is not
"catastrophe." Forgive me.

Washing up on the borders of my solitude,
you appeared upon a screen.

You changed me. Utterly. And now,
in the aftermath,

the self that I became
disseminates an urgency, a nation named by what

it touches, wars against and renders.
This is not an easy task,

but it is, perhaps, the only one: "Listen; Translate;
Speak." We must remember

one another. We must remember. The desert of identity
expands: "We are included"

DENIZEN

"In events the myriad // lights have entered / us it is a music more powerful // than music"
~ George Oppen

1.]

It happens and it occurs. These are our times
happening, their weight and consequence
a noise that cancels out
and others, a noise of war,
of nothingness, which is potentially an act

within its infancy, a thing
through which we make each other
into endings, our edges
pressed together, pulled and parted
open, torn and tortured, that we exist, are still

existing somehow through the fact
of our erasure, beginning over
and again, ceaselessly
and through it. That one is left
no choice but to imagine. No world
but that of words to build a breathing world between us

2.]

Covenant as bridge, "there shall be people." The breath [a kind of noise beyond the
book] transcribes the book
as secular. Between competing points of reference

on the horizon [I, as in
insurgency] like atmosphere at times occurring wildly

in the interior [no sea
or even reason] [leads to a reduction] [a process
by which the state of nation-states surrounds our thinking, enters everything

and ends against
itself] [as land

and circumstance] [as hydrogen, an openness exists

                    if one is listening] [a bond to oxygen]
                        [as bomb] A face beyond

                                   its politic

3.]

It was the month in which the noise became the violence of its occurrence. The garden ended in September and it burned. In "the east" they lit a flag and raised their own above the ashes of our reasoning. Though I was far, I felt responsible. I had done so little to abate the context going on around me. Everywhere around me, a violence flitting in the wind and scattering, a thing. From which arose the structure of a nation which invaded. I felt responsible. The news was everywhere, the war and what to think of it. The thousand threads of it. Which were and are particular, in both a person's hands, peculiar, the fact of continents, estrangement. In the mornings I wrote poetry in a small café and read what lived and died on my computer. Elsewhere, smoke designed its ornaments against the sky. In a valley far away the alphabet became a desert and I crossed it. I found no water there but that which welled in others

4.]

What is thinking now upon atrocity? A thought
discretely gripped around its subject
enters into one of many fields described in art as actual,
none of which approximate an overlap.

This it could be said and has been. Terror
alters us. We speak and are immediate, relating strangely
to the wind which picks the desert up
and changes it. What is carried there, what noise exists

upon announcement, the groundwork
of a correspondence. "I would like to write to you
from deep within the language of a room," some music present
in the tepid depth of these remains, excursions,

a sound within a sound pronounced to live inside of
like a death-thought. Is this excusable?
Do we forgive ourselves too easily? In such a world
as this, at such a distance, it is possible to hear

from deep within the safety of an unexploded building
the continuous expansion and retraction
of the human lung as it attempts
to push and pull the air that others scream in

5.]

Heard at certain distances, the cry of a civilian responding to the sudden and unexpected vacancy of loss begins to take the shape and form of music violently composed. Categories of voices used in the production of human music (and thus our sense of "the human") include "chest voice," "middle voice," "head voice," "whistle voice," "falsetto," and "vocal fry." An irritant known mostly for its pulmonary properties, chlorine gas affects the body through the production of hypochlorous and hydrochloric acid. To perform the vocal fry correctly, one controls the air, taking care, above all else, to stay suspended above a whisper. This occurs when elemental chlorine reacts with water. The song of cells attaching strangely to the edges of the cells around them is one of many sentences in which the verb "to be" begins to disappear upon the instance of its utterance. Agree or disagree. To weep is to belong to that which waits beyond the problem of the singular, there in the impossible despondency of things. Cry of error, the molecular. One is often emptied

6.]

Aesthetically, what defines a desert is a human being
burning in a cage. In the ears of the dead,
music isn't beautiful
or rare. When written in a state
proportionate exactly
to the fact of history invisibly defined, language often shadows
out the other. Histologic findings
of this occurrence include: bronchial
edema, desquamation
of epithelial cells, erosions and localized
necrosis. It is difficult
not to look on Youtube. It is difficult,
but one has done it, often
and repeatedly, varying the angle
of the screen, the time
of day, the music. This damages the cell walls
and negates them, interacting
with various amino and enzyme systems. Speaking
is amiss. This damages the circuitry of the vast
electric happening. Thus, the desert blisters where its edges meet
with thought. How should we compose?

7.]

Every book is a community. Occurring openly. In the desert of the singular, an act of faith or else an orchestra opposed to its arrangement.

From this the poem arises, disseminates a fledgling
self into the air.

Mouths and sand and syllables. A destination leading
to an overwhelming sense

                                        of the particular. Of who we are
                                                            as people

8.]

Of narrative and nationality, a state
of pure emergency. Talk

is occupation.
"Speak to me,

just speak." [The neighbor's house
is burning. Beautiful,

the trees. The trees
existing.] "Master, fuck me harder"

9.]

Moored to this, to them and thus the world
that speaking makes

around us, attached to things
and that from which arises

thingness, the myth of surfaces in the beginning,
occurring over in the aftermath

of time, of populace, becoming nothing
in particular and therefore

more than real, the art of the material
and what to make of it,

what form to struggle
with or for,

that we may be there
differently, again, emerging through an opening,

a doorway in the wilderness,
or mouth

10.]

The course of empire illuminates the path
behinds us. Apathetically the noise

that deafens from the screen
and is, to this extent, commercial

in an ordinary sense, arises
in the middle

distance, a difference between localities
extending out from one place

to another, a bridge it could be said
and has been, most certainly a sound, I hear it

there, it is, I see it, here,
together breathing, you, I see you, are you breathing

11.]

Cage or context or cacophony.
The noise accumulates beyond the mind's ability
to score it. Translation becomes
necessity. The music there
as well as somewhere, existing in the rich
and orchestrated light

of a computer. I am sitting in a room.
Having never had to hear directly
that which does in this world,
not the next, occur. Having eaten well
and exercised and learned. Having written,

having read, what is it then that I exist
within the system of a system
of a system of. Startled, staring out,
not screaming, my voice is not
the voice that I remember happening.
It isn't accurate, the sound

and its appearances. It isn't accurate enough.
Though it occurs within a framework,
a page of snow or else the static overwhelmingly
apparent, a surface scarred by what is written
on it, the shape and shadow of a flag

atop a building, moving in the wind,
its angry history unfurling like the alphabet,
which has been used and put within
the service of atrocity. Which is itself a desert
spoken of and into, a violence made
to make an order, to enforce. O to breathe the air

12.]

Breathing solely into the upper regions of the chest, an untrained vocalist pulls without intention at the air around her body. The first effect is a burning pain in the throat and eyes, followed by suffocation. As a result, the lungs emanate a meager 40 percent of the singer's potential volume. Respiration becomes increasingly difficult as the pain behind the sternum rises. Because the posture of the vocalist is poor. Because vomiting provides relief, the head begins to tilt, reaching for the upper pitches, for the lower. Relief is temporary. The lips and mouth grow parched. The high notes pinch. A thick, dry fur begins to gather on the tongue, a sticky film. Despite the sound that one imagines she is making, the song constricts and hardens. Nothing more is known about cases which prove fatal in the field

13.]

If I have learned to sing I have done so only
as a matter of result.

Language is a residue.
I cling.

At the end of a line of others speaking at the end
of a line of others.

That one can take a sound and make it over
in their image should remind us

beautifully at last
of the appearances

surrounding noises changed to music
and renamed. An image tuned

or turned to face its maker.
Therefore: one must force oneself

to do this, often
and repeatedly, to say as many voices

together mostly, but only
mostly: "Here I am, a variance, a violence"

14.]

Ebbing inward, a drift of energies distends an interruption
in the sense of being noise an impasse makes
of difference. Only causes
are occult. "Eros," or
"the west." A stranger's face
becoming difficult in certain light,
a new desire, terror. It's beginning to feel a lot
like I'm at fault for something
far away. [That there
is television. That I sit within a room.]
Spell apology, spell mercy. I know the world we make
collapses, but the first time I ever read
a poem that worked I got
distracted. The words came in from nowhere
and I agreed. The world came in,
the noise in which it's getting difficult
to pray: to be a part, to separate.
Before the alphabet begins to ache again as series,
even finite now I must
remind myself to say "not faith
so much as what is after
center: other: there." A state of many nations, names,
a strangeness overwhelmingly
apparent, absent. We find it difficult

to mind and cannot say it: "War, the terrible
satisfactions." That we are capable
of this. That finally, after everything, we find that we comply

POSTSCRIPT || NOTES

NOTE ONE It should be noted here at the work's conclusion that a large portion of the language found in *Orient* does not belong to it. Many of the poems in this collection first occurred as the product of a yearlong process of transcription, (mis)translation, erasure, and collage.

NOTE TWO This book could not have been written without the creative and critical efforts of George Oppen, Etel Adnan, Edward Said, Inger Christensen, Lisa Robertson, Robert Baker, Susan Sontag, Maggie Nelson, Simon Weil, Fanny Howe, Brian Eno, and William Basinski, among others.

NOTE THREE "Wherever we are, what we hear is mostly noise. When we ignore it, it disturbs us. When we listen to it, we find it fascinating." – John Cage

NOTE FOUR "Book of Origins" is for my father, Arthur Frederick Gulig, in memorium.

NOTE FIVE "Some Apostasies" is for Jessica Laura Binder, in memorium.

NOTE SIX The majority of the images which recur throughout *Orient* were taken in 2005 by Ian Wallace during an archeological dig in Syria. The ruins depicted show the remains of Palmyra, an ancient Semitic city and world heritage site destroyed by the Islamic State of Iraq and the Levant in 2015. The final image in the book is a photograph of Lake Jean in Quetico Provincial Park, taken by Tony Gulig in the summer of 2016.

NOTE SEVEN "How can we remain beneath a single roof? / When there are seas between us, and walls, deserts of cold ash..." was translated by Mounah A. Khouri and Hamid Algar.

NOTE EIGHT "Through the ear, we shall enter the invisibility of things" was translated by Rosmarie Waldrop.

NOTE NINE The poem "Omphalos" was written in conjunction/conversation with a series of paintings by Janet Waring.

NOTE TEN There was/is a woman I saw interviewed on television to whom I would like to dedicate this book in its entirety. These poems are, in many ways, an inadequate response to a question she posed to a reporter. She was standing in the desert. She held her daughter. I do not know their names.

NOTE ELEVEN "We were walls facing walls / It was painful to talk / It was painful to feel distance / Choked by tragedy / It was painful to talk"

كنا جدراناً أمام جدران

كان مؤلماً أن نتكلم

كان مؤلماً أن نتكلم

كان مؤلماً أن نحس البعد

كان مؤلماً أن نتكلم

— Khalil Hawi
(*trans. by Abdullah al-Udhari*)

ACKNOWLEDGEMENTS || PEOPLE

Thanks is due to the editors of *Omidawn*, *Apartment Poetry*, *Grist*, *jubilat*, and *Like Starlings* where earlier iterations of some of the poems in *Orient* first found homes.

I would also like to thank my parents, Arthur and Shatuporn Gulig, for their love and patience and support, as well as Tony, Oliver, Carla, Brian, and Wesley.

Rich Bell, John Hildebrand, and Dale Peters, thank you.

To my friends and family in Eau Claire, Minneapolis, Missoula, Iowa City, Denver, and Khon Kaen, thank you.

Lifelong debts are owed to Nikolas Novak, Nickolas Butler, and Ian Wallace.

I'd also like to thank Ryan Olson, Justin Vernon, and Drew Christopherson, among others, for making the music of our town and creating our community, for remaining dedicated.

To my teachers, especially Joanna Klink, Robert Baker, James Galvin, Elizabeth Robinson, Dan Beachy-Quick, Rod Smith, Geoffrey G. O'Brien, Graham Foust, Selah Saterstrom, Scott Howard, Eleni Sikelianos, and Laird Hunt, thank you.

For lending your thoughts and voices, Hadara Bar-Nadav, Prageeta Sharma, and Julie Carr, thank you.

Jane Wong, Serena Chopra, Cody Rose Clevidence, Ally Harris, Sara Boyer, Emily Motzkus and Colin Cheney, thank you for your friendship and your influence and support.

A debt is owed as well to my colleagues at the University of Wisconsin-Whitewater, and to the College of Arts and Sciences who provided me the time and money needed to complete this book.

I first began *Orient* after listening to, and speaking with, Dr. Nadar Hashemi of the University of Denver's Joseph Korbel School of International Studies. I would like to thank him here.

An enormous amount of gratitude is owed to Caryl Pagel and Hilary Plum for the attention given to the editing of *Orient*, as well as to the judges of the CSU Poetry Open Book Contest and everyone else at the Cleveland State University Poetry Center who contributed their talent and sacrificed their time.

Finally, and most of all, to my wife Numfon, my daughter Tonkhoa, and to Pieta on the way, my abiding love and admiration. Yours are the lives to which my own life orients most directly. I owe you everything.

RECENT CLEVELAND STATE UNIVERSITY
POETRY CENTER PUBLICATIONS

POETRY

The Hartford Book by Samuel Amadon
The Grief Performance by Emily Kendal Frey
My Fault by Leora Fridman
Stop Wanting by Lizzie Harris
Vow by Rebecca Hazelton
The Tulip-Flame by Chloe Honum
Render / An Apocalypse by Rebecca Gayle Howell
A Boot's a Boot by Lesle Lewis
In One Form to Find Another by Jane Lewty
50 Water Dreams by Siwar Masannat
daughterrarium by Shelia McMullin
The Bees Make Money in the Lion by Lo Kwa Mei-en
Residuum by Martin Rock
Festival by Broc Rossell
The Firestorm by Zach Savich
Mother Was a Tragic Girl by Sandra Simonds
I Live in a Hut by S.E. Smith
Bottle the Bottles the Bottles the Bottles by Lee Upton
Adventures in the Lost Interiors of America by William D. Waltz
Uncanny Valley by Jon Woodward
You Are Not Dead by Wendy Xu

ESSAYS

A Bestiary by Lily Hoang
I Liked You Better Before I Knew You So Well by James Allen Hall

TRANSLATION

I Burned at the Feast: Selected Poems of Arseny Tarkovsky translated by Philip
Metres and Dimitri Psurtsev

For a complete list of titles visit www.csupoetrycenter.com